FROM SEA to SHINING SEA

MICHIGAN

ELIZABETH M. JOHNSON

Consultants

MELISSA N. MATUSEVICH, PH.D.
Curriculum and Instruction Specialist
Blacksburg, Virginia

WENDY S. WOLTJER
Youth Librarian
Kalamazoo Public Library
Kalamazoo, Michigan

M. JILL STREIT
Social Studies Coordinator
Livonia Public Schools
Livonia, Michigan

CHILDREN'S PRESS ®
AN IMPRINT OF SCHOLASTIC INC.

New York · Toronto · London · Auckland · Sydney · Mexico City
New Delhi · Hong Kong · Danbury, Connecticut

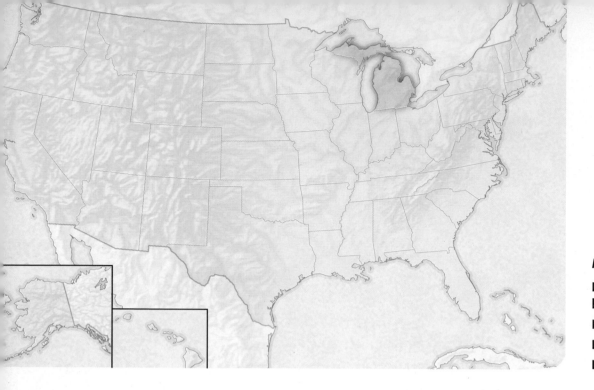

Michigan is in the northern part of the United States. It is bordered by Canada, Wisconsin, Indiana, Ohio, Lake Michigan, Lake Huron, Lake Erie, and Lake Superior.

Project Editor: Meredith DeSousa
Art Director: Marie O'Neill
Photo Researcher: Marybeth Kavanagh
Design: Robin West, Ox and Company, Inc.
Page 6 map and recipe art: Susan Hunt Yule
All other maps: XNR Productions, Inc.

Library of Congress Cataloging in-Publication Data
Johnson, Elizabeth M. (Elizabeth Mary)
    Michigan / by Elizabeth M. Johnson
      p. cm. – (From sea to shining sea)
    Includes bibliographical references and index.
    Summary: Takes the reader on a tour of the state with the longest freshwater
shoreline in the world, emphasizing its geography, history, government, and culture.
    ISBN-10 0-531-21133-9
    ISBN-13 978-0-531-21133-5
    I. Michigan–Juvenile literature. I. Title. II. Series

F566.3 .J63 2009
977.4—dc22   2008020527

TABLE of CONTENTS

CHAPTER ONE

INTRODUCING THE GREAT LAKES STATE

The Holland Harbor Lighthouse, known as "Big Red," is one of more than a hundred lighthouses in Michigan.

Michigan is one of the most easily recognized states. Even astronauts in space looking back at the earth can see this state's familiar mitten shape. People from Michigan often show others where they live by pointing to a spot on their right hand—their very own map of Michigan.

The mitten is only part of Michigan. The state is made up of two peninsulas—land bordered by water on three sides. These two peninsulas give Michigan the longest shoreline of any state except Alaska. No matter where you stand in Michigan, you are never more than 85 miles (137 kilometers) from one of the Great Lakes. Even the word *Michigan* might refer to water. One theory says that *Michigan* comes from the Chippewa word, *michi-gama,* which means "big (or great) water." Others have suggested that it may have come from the Ojibwe (Chippewa) word, *majigan,* which means "clearing."

Michigan touches the lives of many Americans every day, from the cars they drive to the breakfast cereal they eat. The "Big Three" United States automakers—Ford, General Motors, and Chrysler—have their headquarters there. Crops grown in Michigan, such as cherries, blueberries, and apples, can be found in grocery stores around the country. Its factories produce paper products, cereal, baby food, furniture, chemicals, and medicines that people all over the world use every day.

Michigan is also associated with many of our country's famous people. They include Gerald R. Ford, the thirty-eighth president of the United States, and athletes such as basketball great Earvin "Magic" Johnson and the Detroit Tigers' Ty Cobb. Entertainers Aretha Franklin and James Earl Jones are also from Michigan.

What comes to mind when you think of Michigan?

- Tourists riding bicycles on Mackinac Island
- White-tailed deer in the forests
- Ships traveling through Soo Locks on the St. Marys River
- Cherry orchards and delicious cherry pies
- Stately lighthouses by the water
- Skiers flying down the slopes at one of Michigan's many ski resorts

In Michigan there is something for everyone—outdoor activities, history, scenery, sports, and art. It is a state full of beauty and adventure. Read on to find out more about Michigan and all it has to offer.

LAKE SUPERIOR

Ontario Canada

©SHY01

Marquette

LAKE HURON

Wisconsin

LAKE MICHIGAN

Illinois

Grand
Rapids

Lansing

Flint

Ann Arbor

Canada

Sterling Heights

Detroit

LAKE ERIE

Indiana

Ohio

CHAPTER TWO

THE LAND OF MICHIGAN

According to a Native American legend, the world was once covered with water. The great turtle, Michilimackinac, let the other animals rest on his broad back when they got tired of swimming. Over time he grew old and wanted to give his friends a gift before he died. So he asked the animals to dive to the bottom of the lake and bring up a pawful of earth. One after another the friends tried, and finally Muskrat brought up a clod of soil and placed it on the turtle's back. Slowly, the land began to cover the turtle's back and it became a large island, shaped like a giant turtle. And so the island of Mackinac was born.

If you look at Mackinac Island, near the point where the upper and lower peninsulas meet, you'll see that it does indeed look like a large turtle. It wasn't a magic turtle, however, that formed Michigan's two peninsulas and many islands. It was volcanoes and glaciers (huge, slow-moving sheets of ice). Two million years ago, glaciers pushed south across

The Lake of the Clouds flows through the hills of Porcupine Mountains State Park.

what is now Canada and the United States. As they crossed the land, the glaciers dug holes in the earth that became the Great Lakes. They also created thousands of smaller lakes.

Michigan is made up of two peninsulas—the Upper Peninsula, which is the northern part, and the Lower Peninsula, the southern part. The peninsulas are surrounded by water on three sides and are separated by the Straits of Mackinac, a narrow passage that connects Lake Michigan and Lake Huron. There are two geographic regions in the state: the Superior Upland and the Central Lowland.

Many people enjoy camping in Michigan's mountains.

SUPERIOR UPLAND

The Superior Upland region covers the western half of the Upper Peninsula. This area is rugged, with many hills and forests.

Volcanoes and other changes inside the earth created the Porcupine and Huron mountain ranges in the western Upper Peninsula. They are the only mountain ranges between the Allegheny Mountains in the eastern United States and the Rocky Mountains in the west. The highest

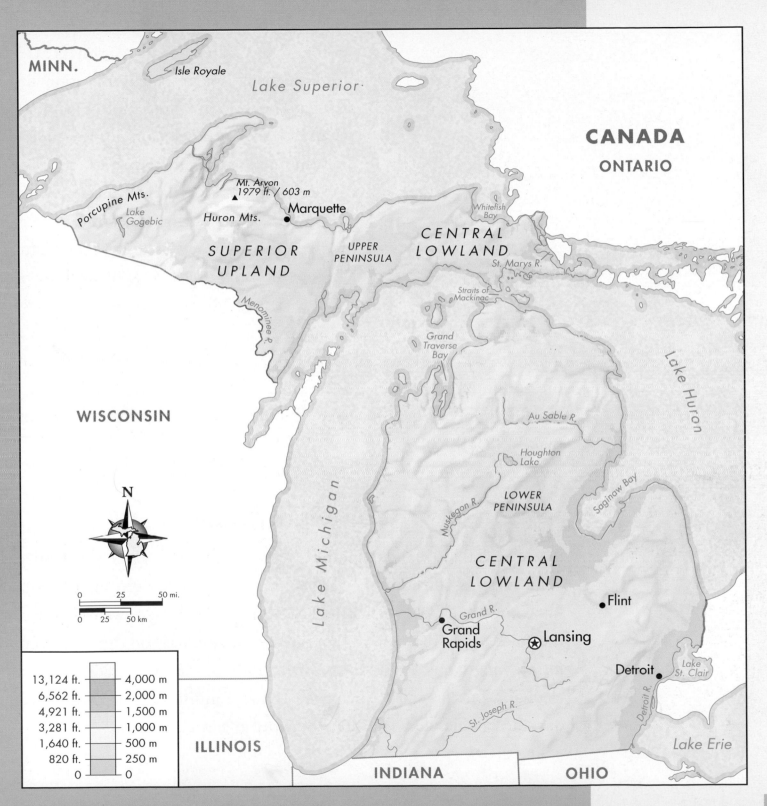

MINN.

Isle Royale

Lake Superior

CANADA

ONTARIO

Porcupine Mts.

*Lake
Gogebic*

Mt. Arvon
1979 ft. / 603 m

▲

Huron Mts.

● Marquette

Whitefish
Bay

SUPERIOR
UPLAND

UPPER
PENINSULA

CENTRAL
LOWLAND

St. Marys R.

Menominee R.

Straits of
Mackinac

Grand
Traverse
Bay

Lake Huron

WISCONSIN

Au Sable R.

*Houghton
Lake*

Lake Michigan

Muskegon R.

LOWER
PENINSULA

Saginaw Bay

N

CENTRAL
LOWLAND

● Flint

0   25   50 mi.

0   25   50 km

Grand R.

● Grand
Rapids

⊛ Lansing

Detroit ●

*Lake
St. Clair*

13,124 ft.	4,000 m
6,562 ft.	2,000 m
4,921 ft.	1,500 m
3,281 ft.	1,000 m
1,640 ft.	500 m
820 ft.	250 m
0	0

Detroit R.

St. Joseph R.

ILLINOIS

Lake Erie

INDIANA

OHIO

point in the state, Mount Arvon (1,979 feet/603 meters), is in the Huron Mountain Range. The western Upper Peninsula is part of the Canadian Shield, one of the oldest rock formations in North America.

This region is rich in minerals, with some of the nation's largest deposits of iron and copper. Iron ore was discovered in the Upper Peninsula in 1844. William Burt, a surveyor who was responsible for setting Michigan's boundary lines, found underground iron deposits by accident when his compass needle began to jerk uncontrollably because of iron's magnetic properties. Iron ore continues to be mined today and is used in manufacturing. Nonmetallic mineral resources that are mined include limestone (used to make cement), salt, and gypsum.

CENTRAL LOWLAND

The Central Lowland region covers the eastern half of the Upper Peninsula and the entire Lower Peninsula. The Lower Peninsula is also known as the Michigan Basin. Thousands of years ago, water covered the land. When the water disappeared, it left behind soil that was good for growing crops. Mastodons and mammoths, ancient relatives of the elephant, once roamed Michigan's Lower Peninsula. When they died out, their bodies decayed and also helped to enrich the soil.

The Lower Peninsula has miles of sandy shoreline, including Sleeping Bear Dunes National Lakeshore. This is a 35-mile (56-kilometer) stretch of sand dunes along Lake Michigan. According to Native American legend, a mother bear swam across Lake Michigan with her two cubs to escape a forest fire. She reached shore, but the cubs did not. As she waited and watched for them atop a hill, she was covered with sand and became a great dune. Her cubs, who drowned, became the North and South Manitou Islands.

Pictured Rocks National Lakeshore is on the Upper Peninsula along Lake Superior. This area of sandstone cliffs was created by the movement of glaciers. Glaciers also created many waterfalls. As glaciers traveled they eroded, or wore away, layers of rock, leaving behind large valleys. Later, when rivers flowed through the area, they eroded the top layer of soft rock and plunged over into the valley below. Today there are nearly 150 beautiful waterfalls in this region.

Pictured Rocks National Lakeshore is named for the Pictured Rocks, which rise up from the lake to heights of up to 200 feet (60 m).

Petroleum and natural gas are found in parts of the Lower Peninsula. Aboveground, timber is one of Michigan's greatest natural resources. More than half the state is covered in forest, including white pine, the state tree. Many varieties of trees grow in Michigan—oak, hickory, maple, beech, elm, ash, spruce, and cedar. Fruit trees, including cherry and apple trees, also grow in Michigan.

LAKES AND RIVERS

"Water, water everywhere" would be a good state motto, because one is never more than six miles (10 km) from a lake or river in Michigan. In fact, "Water Wonderland" is one of Michigan's nicknames. The state has 3,288 miles (5,290 km) of shore-line, a length greater than the entire Atlantic coast of the United States.

Michigan borders on four of the five Great Lakes—Lake Huron, Lake Superior, Lake Michigan, and Lake Erie. In addition to the Great Lakes, which are used for shipping, boating, fishing, and much more, Michigan has more than eleven thousand smaller lakes. Some of its larger lakes

Sailboats are a common sight on Lake Michigan.

include Houghton, Torch, and Crystal Lakes in the Lower Peninsula, and Lake Gogebic in the Upper Peninsula.

The 260-mile (418-km) Grand River is Michigan's longest river. It winds through central Michigan and empties into Lake Michigan at Grand Haven. Rivers such as the Muskegon in the west and Au Sable in the east were used for sending logs from forests to sawmills in the early days. The St. Marys River, Detroit River, and St. Clair River make it possible for cargo ships to travel between the Great Lakes, carrying natural resources and manufactured products from Michigan to the rest of the world.

CLIMATE

Michigan has mild springs, warm summers, crisp autumns, and snowy winters. Moisture from the surrounding bodies of water creates lots of rain, sleet, hail, and even blizzards. Winds from the lakes create clouds, resulting in lots of overcast days in the Great Lakes state.

A condition called "lake effect" makes winter weather along the shore very different from the weather inland. In the winter, cold air settles over warm water in the Great Lakes, creating clouds. The clouds turn into snow, and blowing winds cause "lake effect" snow to fall in the areas around the lake.

The Lower Peninsula has milder weather than the Upper Peninsula, which has fierce

FIND OUT MORE

Michigan's temperate climate, particularly in the southwest, is perfect for growing fruit such as cherries and apples. How do you think Lake Michigan affects the climate in this area and helps to create a good growing season?

storms and freezing winters. July temperatures range from 58° to 75°F (14° to 24°C) in the Upper Peninsula and 63° to 84°F (17° to 29°C) in the Lower Peninsula. January temperatures range from 10° to 25°F (−12° to −4°C) in the Upper Peninsula and 19° to 32°F (−7° to 0°C) in the Lower Peninsula.

Detroit, in the Lower Peninsula, averages 30 to 40 inches (76 to 102 centimeters) of snow per year. In contrast, the Upper Peninsula's Keweenaw Peninsula—the northernmost point in Michigan—averages 250 to 300 inches (635 to 762 cm) of snow each year. The record annual snowfall in the state was 391.9 inches (995 cm), recorded in Delaware during the winter of 1978–1979. That's almost deep enough to bury a school bus that's been stood on end!

In the winter, snowplows are a familiar sight, especially in the Upper Peninsula.

CHAPTER THREE

MICHIGAN THROUGH HISTORY

This drawing shows a freighter traveling through a lock in Sault Ste. Marie.

(opposite)
Early Native Americans hunted and fished along the shores of Lake Superior.

Imagine a land where mastodons and woolly mammoths roamed, where giant beavers built dams and elk and muskoxen grazed among tall pine trees. This was the area known as Michigan before people arrived. The first people, hunters from the north, found Michigan and its rich land nearly ten thousand years ago. These early people hunted, fished, and lived on the berries and wild rice that grew there. Some were mining copper in the Upper Peninsula as long ago as 3000 B.C., making the first metal weapons and tools in the New World.

After 500 B.C., more people came into the area. One group of Native Americans was called the Hopewell. They built large mounds on the land using earth, stone, and other materials. The mounds were most likely used as burial places, and may have also served as religious temples. In 1874, scientists dug up seventeen mounds near the city of Grand Rapids.

They ranged in size from 30 feet (9 m) across and 18 inches (46 cm) high to 100 feet (30 m) across and 15 feet (5 m) high. Eleven of these mounds have been preserved so that people today can study the culture of these Native Americans who lived more than two thousand years ago.

By the time the first Europeans came to Michigan, the land was home to three main tribes of Native Americans. Together, they were known as the People of the Three Fires: the Ojibwe (Chippewa), the Odawa (Ottawa), and the Potawatomi. The Ojibwe were a fishing tribe who lived mainly in the eastern Upper Peninsula. The Odawa were traders who lived in the western parts of the Lower Peninsula. These groups wandered from place to place, traveling on rivers and lakes. The Potawatomi lived in villages in the southwest, where they grew corn, beans, and squash. Another group, the Huron (Wyandot), lived in the southeast, near present-day Detroit. The Miami lived in southern Michigan, and the Menominee lived in parts of the Upper Peninsula.

EXTRA! EXTRA!

In the 1800s, explorers found the remains of ancient copper pits in the northern Upper Peninsula and on Isle Royale, an island in Lake Superior. Their discovery indicates that early Native Americans were the first people to find and mine copper in the western Upper Peninsula, making them the first metalworkers in North America. These ancient people heated the copper with fire to soften it, then chipped away at it with stone hammers. People in Michigan have found copper tools, spear tips, and knives more than three thousand years old.

The first Europeans to set foot in Michigan were French explorers. Samuel de Champlain, the governor of New France (Canada), sent explorer Étienne Brûlé to find a trade route to China or India. About 1618, Brûlé and his crew arrived in the eastern Upper Peninsula. Another French explorer, Jean Nicolet, also set out at the direction of Champlain. He sailed through the Straits of Mackinac into Lake Michigan, and came ashore near Green Bay, Wisconsin. Neither of these explorers found a route to China, but they did find something else—a land rich with fur-bearing animals. At that time, people in France and other European countries paid a lot of money for fancy clothing and hats made from animal furs and skins.

The French hunted animals for their skins, or pelts. They also traded with the Native Americans, who were skilled hunters and could get animal skins quickly and easily. In exchange, the French gave them tools, weapons, and cloth. French traders, called voyageurs, traveled in canoes up to 40 feet (12 m) long that could carry hun-

Native Americans traded with the French for goods such as cloth, tools, and weapons.

WHO'S WHO IN MICHIGAN?

Father Jacques Marquette (1637–1675) was a French priest who came to Michigan to teach Native Americans about Christianity. He founded the missions of Sault Ste. Marie in 1668 and St. Ignace in 1671, both on the Upper Peninsula.

dreds of animal skins to trading posts along the Great Lakes. Often, missionary priests traveled with the explorers and traders to bring the Christian religion to Native Americans. In 1668, the first European settlement in Michigan was established at Sault Ste. Marie by Father Jacques Marquette, a Jesuit missionary.

French nobleman Antoine de La Mothe, Sieur de Cadillac, came to Michigan after convincing the French king that the land would be a good place for French people to settle. He founded a trading post called Fort Pontchartrain (which later became known as La Ville d'Etroit or modern-day Detroit) in the Lower Peninsula in 1701. The French also built Fort Michilimackinac overlooking the Straits of Mackinac in 1715. These two forts were fur trading centers and important military outposts.

The trading business was so successful it also attracted the British. Throughout the 1700s and into the 1800s, the French, the British, and the Native Americans fought for control of the forts. During the French and Indian War (1754–1763), the British fought the French for control of Michigan and other parts of North America. Native Americans helped the French because they feared that the British would take over their land. In 1760, the British gained control of North America east of the Mississippi River, including Michigan.

By this time, Native Americans in Michigan and Ohio were weary of Europeans' interference in their lives. In an effort to fight back, Native Americans attacked three major forts in 1763. Ojibwe fighters attacked the British at Fort Michilimackinac. In the west, Potawatomi warriors captured Fort St. Joseph, in present-day Niles. In the southeast, warriors from the Ottawa tribe, led by Chief Pontiac, attempted to take Detroit by surprise. They were unable to do so, but they kept the fort under siege for about 134 days. This meant that no one could leave the fort and no supplies could get into the fort. However, the British eventually regained control of all three forts. These attacks were part of what is known as Pontiac's Rebellion.

THE END OF BRITISH RULE

After the French and Indian War, Britain had complete control over the region. They continued fur trading, which was still very profitable. The British discouraged any new settlement in the interior of Michigan for fear of disrupting the trading business.

Meanwhile, many colonists in the east were not satisfied living under British rule. They felt that many of Britain's laws were unfair, and they resented being ruled by a country more than three thousand miles away. The colonists wanted to be independent.

Tension grew between the colonists and the British. In 1775, the American Revolution (1775–1783) began. Most of the fighting took place in the east, so the war had little immediate effect on Michigan, which was sparsely populated. Even though the colonies defeated the British in 1783, the British refused to leave the forts in Michigan because they were important centers for trade and power. It wasn't until 1796—thirteen years after the war was over—that the United States army finally forced the British to leave Michigan.

MICHIGAN TERRITORY

After the war, Michigan became part of the United States, but it was not yet a state. In 1787, the U.S. government created the Northwest Territory, which contained all its lands north of the Ohio River and east of the Mississippi River. In 1800, Michigan became part of the smaller Indiana Territory. In 1805, Michigan Territory was formed.

A huge celebration took place upon the official opening of the Erie Canal.

FIND OUT MORE

Draw a map of New York state and label the Hudson River, Lake Erie, Albany, Buffalo, and the neighboring state of Michigan. Then trace the route of the Erie Canal from beginning to end, showing how the canal helped people and products to reach Michigan.

Although more people moved to the area, Michigan didn't really begin to grow until the Erie Canal opened in 1825. This canal created a water route that linked the Hudson River in New York with Lake Erie on Michigan's eastern border. A trip that used to take thirty days by wagon now took fourteen days traveling the Erie Canal. Settlers from New York, Pennsylvania, and other northeastern states came to Michigan because they heard about Michigan's fertile farmland. The canal also made it easier to transport products such as food crops, lumber, and iron ore. These items could now be sent to cities in the east.

Michigan had nine thousand settlers in 1820. In 1830, five years after the Erie Canal opened, "Michigan Fever" erupted and the number of settlers increased to 31,640. In another ten years, the population had grown to more than two hundred thousand. The state continued to grow as immigrants from Finland, Norway, the Netherlands, Germany, and England arrived to work in Michigan's industries such as mining and lumbering.

Men, women, and children crowded onto ships bound for Michigan. They came from Germany, Finland, Britain, the Netherlands, and other countries.

As settlers moved in, Native Americans living in Michigan were pushed further west. The United States government made treaties (formal agreements) with the Native Americans, offering them money in exchange for large areas of native territories. The government forced them to live in smaller areas called reservations, which would be owned by each tribe. Native Americans kept their right to hunt and fish on the land they had sold to the United States.

WHO'S WHO IN MICHIGAN?

Stevens T. Mason (1811–1843) was appointed territorial secretary of Michigan by President Andrew Jackson when he was just nineteen years old. He led Michigan to statehood by conducting an official census of the area in 1834 and calling the first constitutional convention. The people of Michigan elected him to be their first governor in 1835, though Michigan wouldn't be recognized as a state until 1837.

(opposite)
Thomas Edison's invention of the electric light bulb sparked interest in the Upper Peninsula, where copper (a mineral that conducts electricity) was mined.

Despite this, white settlers often broke the treaties and took land that was given to the Native Americans. Soon, most of the state's Native American population was located only in the Upper Peninsula, Grand Traverse Bay, and Mt. Pleasant areas. These lands were important tribal hunting grounds and settlements for the tribes that lived there, and they did not want to move further west. Between 1650 and 1900, Michigan's Native American population declined from one hundred thousand to just eight thousand.

STATEHOOD

By the mid-1830s, Michigan had enough residents to apply for statehood. In 1835, Michigan held its first constitutional convention from May 11 to June 24, where it was decided that Detroit would be the state capital. Also, Michigan's first constitution, a document outlining the organization of the state's government, was drafted.

It took eighteen months for the United States government to approve Michigan's statehood because of a disagreement between Michigan and the state of Ohio. The argument was about the ownership of a 500-square mile (1,295-sq km) strip of land that included Toledo. The disagreement, often referred to as the "Toledo War," ended when the federal government gave the Toledo Strip to Ohio, and the Upper Peninsula to Michigan. On January 26, 1837, Michigan became the 26th state. Detroit served as the capital until 1847, when the capital was moved to Lansing.

To the surprise of most Michiganians, the Upper Peninsula held valuable treasures. A Michigan geologist, Douglass Houghton, discovered copper on the Keweenaw Peninsula in 1841. His discovery set off a mining boom in the Upper Peninsula. The area turned out to be full of copper, iron ore, and timber. In the 1800s, copper was used to make pots and pans, coins, roofing material, ship bottoms, brass, and gun metal. When Thomas Edison invented the electric light bulb, copper became even more valuable because it conducts electricity. In the 1870s, half the copper mined in the Upper Peninsula was used in the electrical industry.

Mining was highly successful, but miners now needed a better way to move iron

25

WHAT'S IN A NAME?

Many names and places in Michigan have unusual origins or reflect the state's history.

Name	Comes from or means
Detroit	"Ville d'Etroit," French for "town of the straits"
Mason	Stevens T. Mason, first elected governor
Houghton Lake	Douglass Houghton, nineteenth-century geologist
Pontiac	Native American leader
Novi	Number 6 (No. VI) stagecoach stop on the road from Detroit; or, the Latin word for "new"
Marquette	Father Jacques Marquette, French missionary

ore from western Michigan to the iron and steel centers along the Great Lakes. The St. Marys River was the only connection between Lake Superior and the lower Great Lakes, but it was not passable for boats because of a 21-foot (6-m) drop on one section of the river. To enable boats to pass through, the State Lock was built in 1855. The lock consisted of a chamber that raised and lowered water levels, carrying ships up or down. It allowed ships to easily come and go on the St. Marys River. Later, the lock became so important to commerce that new locks, called the Soo Locks, were built and operated by the United States government.

SLAVERY AND THE CIVIL WAR

As Michigan was becoming a state, the rest of the country continued to develop. North and South, however, were growing in different ways. In the South, farming was the main source of income, and many people managed large farms called plantations. These plantations ran on the forced labor of enslaved Africans. Enslaved Africans were not citizens. They had few rights and were considered inferior to their white enslavers. Black slaves were "owned" by their white masters, who often treated them harshly. Enslaved Africans were not allowed to travel freely, or to learn to read or write, and could be tortured or killed for trying to escape.

In the North, both blacks and whites worked in factories where they were paid wages. Many Northerners believed slavery was wrong. The northern states eventually made it illegal to enslave Africans within their borders. As new states in the west joined the union, some were admitted as "free" states—states where slavery was not allowed—while others were admitted as "slave" states.

The rules of the Northwest Territory had made Michigan a slavery-free area back in 1787. Many of the settlers who came to Michigan from New York and New England were abolitionists, people who spoke out against slavery. They worked to free Africans and change the laws that made slavery legal in the southern states. Laura Haviland and Sojourner Truth were well-known Michigan abolitionists.

Because of its nearness to Canada (where slavery was not allowed), Michigan was an important stop on the Underground Railroad, a secret chain of people and hiding places. Africans used the Underground Railroad to travel safely to northern states and Canada. Often, people would come to Michigan in search of escaped Africans. In 1847, bounty hunters tracked down Adam Crosswhite, an African who had escaped

from Kentucky and was living with his family in Marshall, Michigan. The people of Marshall protected Crosswhite and threatened to attack the bounty hunters if they didn't get out of town. The bounty hunters left, and Crosswhite remained free, fleeing safely to Canada.

The southern states knew that President Abraham Lincoln wanted to end slavery. In protest they decided to secede, or leave the United States and become their own nation called the Confederate States of America. In 1861, North and South went to war. The states that remained loyal to the United States were known as the Union.

In the Civil War (1861–1865), Michigan fought on the side of the Union, which opposed slavery. Michigan sent ninety thousand soldiers to fight in the war, and about fifteen thousand died. Michigan also supplied food from its abundant crops as well as lumber and iron ore for making buildings and weapons.

WHO'S WHO IN MICHIGAN?

Sarah Emma Edmonds (1841–1898) of Flint fought in the Civil War by disguising herself as a man. She registered for the Army as Franklin Thompson and served with the Second Michigan Volunteer Infantry for two years. She was also a spy for the Union Army. In 1863, she deserted the army so that her true identity would not be discovered. She served as a nurse until the end of the Civil War.

After the Civil War, Michigan's logging industry was booming. As Americans began to settle lands west of the Mississippi River, Michigan supplied lumber to build new homes and towns. After the Great Chicago Fire in 1871, Michigan supplied lumber to rebuild the city. Railroads were built to allow year-round transportation of logs to sawmills and buyers throughout the country.

By 1900, Michigan loggers had cut 161 billion board feet of pine logs and 50 billion board feet of hardwood. Many areas were stripped of trees and the remaining debris was often burned to clear the land. In 1881, after a hot, dry summer, some of these fires burned out of control. That year, fires in the Thumb area of Michigan killed three hundred people.

The lumbering boom brought a new wave of immigrants from Scandinavia, Germany, Ireland, and Canada. Between 1870 and 1900, Michigan's population doubled. Railroad and steamship line operators in Michigan saw a way to profit from the state's newfound popularity. To make more money, they encouraged people to take vacations at Michigan's resorts, such as Mackinac Island. Michigan

In the 1800s, logs were loaded onto carts and brought to a river, where they were sent downstream to the nearest sawmill.

beaches and forests were advertised as a place to get away from the hot, noisy city. People also came to Michigan to visit the sanitarium, or health resort, run by brothers John Harvey and Will Kellogg in Battle Creek in the late 1800s. The Kelloggs experimented with "health foods," and later invented corn flakes, a new breakfast food. C.W. Post, who had been a patient at the sanitarium, also started a breakfast cereal company in Battle Creek.

Guests at the Kellogg brothers' health resort took part in a group exercise regimen.

THE INDUSTRIAL REVOLUTION

Michigan was quickly becoming an important manufacturing center. Michigan factories made and shipped stoves, railroad cars, furniture, drugs, shoes, and many other goods. In fact, Michigan led the country in making iron stoves and railroad cars. Soon, Michigan became associated with a new product, the automobile. Ransom E. Olds in Lansing and Henry Ford in Detroit both developed cars in the 1890s. Olds started the first automobile company, Olds Motor Works, in 1897. He also developed the assembly line, which made the production process faster. In 1903, Henry Ford improved the assembly line method. His assembly line was made up of workers stationed along a conveyor belt. Car bodies were placed on the conveyor belt and each worker added parts as the car moved down the line. Rather than one worker putting together an entire car, each worker was responsible for just one part. The creation of the assembly line allowed Ford to produce more cars in a shorter time.

Ford paid workers five dollars a day—double the standard rate—to work on his assembly line. He also cut the working day by one hour. These revolutionary steps brought thousands of workers from southern states and from other countries into Michigan. Michigan quickly became the country's center of automobile manufacturing.

World War I (1914–1918) began when Germany declared war on Russia and France. The United States did not join the war at the begin-

This man is riding an early version of the Olds Curved Dash, one of the most popular cars in the country in the early 1900s.

FIND OUT MORE

Before Ford introduced the assembly line, it took twelve hours to make one car. With the assembly line, it was possible to put a car together in just ninety minutes. How many more cars could be made in a twelve-hour shift using the assembly line?

ning, but factories all over the country, including those in Michigan, began making products to help fight the Germans. Automobile factories also made trucks, armored vehicles, and airplane engines for the war. In 1917, after Germany attacked several ships carrying Americans, the United States joined the war. More than 135,000 people from Michigan fought in the war.

THE GREAT DEPRESSION AND WORLD WAR II

In 1929, the United States entered the Great Depression (1929–1939). Many people lost money in the stock market, and could no longer afford to buy things they needed. As a result, businesses did poorly and many of them closed, leaving thousands of people without jobs. The remaining workers made little money. Often, people couldn't afford to keep their homes or even buy food. Michigan relied heavily on industry, and as a result it was hit hard by the Great Depression. People could not afford to buy cars and automobile factories laid off many workers.

To help people who lost their jobs, President Franklin D. Roosevelt started many work programs as part of his "New Deal." One New Deal program was the Civilian Conservation Corps (CCC), an organization that put people to work on various public service projects. In Michigan, more than one hundred thousand people worked in the Corps, planting trees, fighting fires, and building parks. By the time the program ended in 1942, workers had planted more than 484 million seedlings, placed 150 million fish in rivers and lakes, and constructed 7,000 miles (11,265 km) of trails, 504 buildings, and 222 bridges in Michigan.

The workers who stayed at the automobile factories worked long hours for little pay. They had no say in how the factory was operated and they could be fired at any time and for any reason. Often, factory owners didn't care whether workers were hurt on the job. Some workers were angry about these unfair working conditions and joined labor unions. A union is a group of workers that joins together to demand better treatment at work.

During the Depression, people who could not afford to buy food went to soup kitchens, where they could get food for free.

One of the most important labor unions, the United Auto Workers, was founded in Michigan. In 1936, auto workers at the General Motors factory in Flint went on strike. They sat down in the factory and refused to work until the owners talked with them and agreed to treat the workers better. The strike was successful and working conditions began to improve.

In 1941 the United States entered World War II, which helped Michigan pull out of the Great Depression. Michigan factories made wartime products such as B-24 bombers, tanks, guns, artillery, torpedoes, and ammunition. The Willow Run plant, operated by Ford Motor Company, built more than 8,500 planes. The Warren Tank Plant, which

Michigan contributed to the success of World War II by producing B-24 bombers, which were used to help fight the war.

made cars for the Chrysler Motor Company, made 25,000 tanks. Detroit's Gibson Refrigerator Company produced airplane engines. Detroit's contributions to the war effort were so great that it was said, "America's (battles) were won on the assembly lines of Detroit." Thousands of women worked on these assembly lines because so many men were fighting in Europe and the Pacific Ocean.

FAMOUS FIRSTS

- First commercially produced soda pop, Vernor's Ginger Ale, 1866
- First telephone numbers assigned to local residents, 1879
- First international underwater railway tunnel—the Grand Trunk Western Railroad tunnel—connected Port Huron and Canada, 1891
- World's first stretch of paved concrete road, Detroit's Woodward Avenue, 1909
- First three-color traffic lights were hung in Detroit, 1920
- Michigan State Police developed the first state police radio system in the world, 1929

AFRICAN-AMERICAN STRUGGLES

The 1950s brought good economic times to Michigan. People bought more cars and other products made in Michigan. The state also became a popular vacation spot, especially after 1957, when the Mackinac Bridge was completed. This bridge linked the lower and upper peninsulas, making it possible to drive from one part of the state to the other instead of taking a ferry.

Business was booming in Michigan, and workers were needed. Many African Americans moved to Michigan from the South to work in the factories. Some white employers hired them reluctantly, but laws were passed that required fair hiring practices.

Detroit, in particular, was a site of racial tension between African Americans and whites. In many parts of the country, African Americans were not viewed as equal to whites, and they were often treated poorly. In Detroit, real estate agents refused to sell them houses in certain neighborhoods, and some apartment owners would not rent them apartments. Banks wouldn't lend money to African Americans, making it even more difficult for them to buy homes. As a result, they were often crowded into low-income areas of the city.

Some African Americans became angry about this unfair treatment and started riots, or violent protests. In July 1967, Detroit riots lasted a week, leaving forty-three people dead and causing millions of dollars in property damage. The Detroit riots led to the Michigan Fair Housing Act, passed in 1968. This law made it illegal to refuse to rent or sell houses to people because of their race. A national law called the Fair Housing Act was also passed in 1968 to prevent discrimination in the sale or rental of housing.

African-American workers forge a piece of hot metal in one of Michigan's factories.

The Michigan National Guard was called out to help control the Detroit riots in 1967.

MODERN MICHIGAN

The auto industry suffered some hard times in the 1970s. A shortage of gasoline caused many people to buy foreign cars that used fuel more efficiently. By the 1980s, the auto industry had recovered.

As Michigan entered the twenty-first century, the economy was once again prospering. Many immigrant groups, including Hispanics, Arabs, and Asians, chose to settle in Michigan. In the 1990s, high-technology industries developed in the southeastern part of the state as people began using computers to design new cars. This "high-tech corridor" attracts people seeking new jobs.

Biotechnology, which uses science to make new medicines, find cures for diseases, and create fruits and vegetables that grow better, is another new industry in Michigan today. Scientists and researchers come to southeastern Michigan to work on biotechnology projects at Michigan State University and the University of Michigan. Michigan ranks eleventh in the nation in biotechnology jobs.

In the 1990s, Michiganians turned their attention to the environment. In 1998, Michigan adopted the Clean Michigan Initiative. As part of this program, money is being spent to improve state parks, clean up lakes and streams, and restore contaminated land to its original state. The protection of their natural resources is important to the people of Michigan.

Michigan State University attracts students and researchers interested in agricultural biotechnology.

FIND OUT MORE

Put together a time capsule for future Michiganians. What will you put in it? Write a letter that will go in the time capsule. What will you say to the people of the future?

In 2001, at the beginning of the twenty-first century, Detroit celebrated its 300th anniversary. Throughout the year, Detroit held special events to honor Antoine de La Mothe, Sieur de Cadillac, who founded Detroit in 1701. The city also celebrated its achievements of the past three hundred years. Once a small French fort, Detroit has become the largest foreign trade zone in the United States today—more than $24 billion in goods leave Detroit for the rest of the world every year. Half of all the trade between the United States and Canada goes through Detroit. The city still remains the center of the car industry, with new designs and better cars being introduced every year.

On New Year's Day 2001, Detroit Mayor Dennis Archer opened a time capsule sealed by the city's then mayor, William C. Maybury, on December 31, 1900. Inside the capsule was a letter that stated, "We communicate by telegraph and telephone over distances that, at the opening of the nineteenth century, seemed insurmountable. . . .We travel by railroad and steam power from Detroit to Chicago in less than eight hours, and to New York City by several routes in less than twenty hours. How much faster are you traveling? . . . We talk by long distance telephone to the remotest cities in our own country, and with a fair degree of practical success. Are you talking to foreign lands and to the island of the sea by the same method?" Mayor Maybury would surely be impressed with today's Michigan, where cars drive at seventy miles (113 km) per hour, people communicate nearly instantly by e-mail, and jet airplanes fly from Detroit to Chicago and New York in just a few hours.

CHAPTER FOUR

GOVERNING MICHIGAN

Michigan is governed according to its constitution, a document that outlines the organization of the state government and also defines the rights of Michigan citizens. Michigan's original constitution was written in 1835, in preparation for statehood, which was granted in 1837. The original constitution was modeled after the United States Constitution. Over time, the people of Michigan have made amendments, or changes, to their constitution, and it has been updated three times—in 1850, 1908, and 1963. Today, Michigan still uses the 1963 constitution.

The organization of Michigan's government is similar to that of the United States government. It has three parts, or branches: the executive, legislative, and judicial. Each branch has different responsibilities, so that no one part has too much power.

The Michigan state capitol was built in 1879. Since then, it has served as a model for the design of many other capitol buildings.

EXECUTIVE BRANCH

The executive branch enforces and carries out state laws. The head of the executive branch is the governor. The governor is elected by the people of Michigan to serve a four-year term in office, and he or she can be reelected two terms in a row for up to eight years. The governor helps bring new jobs and companies to Michigan and works with other elected and appointed state officials to make sure that the state runs smoothly. He or she can veto bills that are passed by the legislative branch and refuse to sign them into law. The governor is also in charge of the state's military forces and can call its soldiers into action to protect and help Michiganians during an emergency.

The people of Michigan also elect the lieutenant governor, the secretary of state, and the attorney general. The governor appoints other people to lead state departments, such as the department of education, the department of transportation, and the department of agriculture.

LEGISLATIVE BRANCH

The legislative branch creates new state laws. Like the federal government, the state legislature has two houses: the senate and the house of representatives. The senate has 38 members and the house of representatives has 110 members. State senators are elected for a four-year term. Representatives serve a two-year term.

MICHIGAN GOVERNORS

Name	Term	Name	Term
Stevens T. Mason	1837–1840	Aaron T. Bliss	1901–1904
William Woodbridge	1840–1841	Fred M. Warner	1905–1910
James Wright Gordon	1841–1842	Chase S. Osborn	1911–1912
John S. Barry	1842–1846	Woodbridge N. Ferris	1913–1916
Alpheus Felch	1846–1847	Albert E. Sleeper	1917–1920
William L. Greenly	1847	Alexander J. Groesbeck	1921–1926
Epaphroditus Ransom	1848–1850	Fred W. Green	1927–1930
John S. Barry	1850–1851	Wilber M. Brucker	1931–1932
Robert McClelland	1852–1853	William A. Comstock	1933–1934
Andrew Parsons	1853–1854	Frank D. Fitzgerald	1935–1936
Kinsley S. Bingham	1855–1858	Frank Murphy	1937–1938
Moses Wisner	1859–1860	Frank D. Fitzgerald	1939
Austin Blair	1861–1864	Luren D. Dickinson	1939–1940
Henry H. Crapo	1865–1868	Murray D. Van Wagoner	1941–1942
Henry P. Baldwin	1869–1872	Harry F. Kelly	1943–1946
John J. Bagley	1873–1876	Kim Sigler	1947–1948
Charles M. Croswell	1877–1880	G. Mennen Williams	1949–1960
David H. Jerome	1881–1882	John B. Swainson	1961–1962
Josiah W. Begole	1883–1884	George Romney	1963–1969
Russell A. Alger	1885–1886	William G. Milliken	1969–1983
Cyrus G. Luce	1887–1890	James J. Blanchard	1983–1991
Edwin B. Winans	1891–1892	John M. Engler	1991–2003
John T. Rich	1893–1896	Jennifer Granholm	2003–
Hazen S. Pingree	1897–1900		

The legislature passes laws and votes on issues that are important to the people of Michigan. They might pass laws to build new schools, clean up the environment, or promote safety in vehicles and homes. Michigan's legislature meets in Lansing.

JUDICIAL BRANCH

The judicial branch interprets the state's laws using a system of courts and judges. Many cases begin in district court. District courts hear cases involving less than $25,000. The next level of courts are circuit courts, which hear civil cases (cases in which two parties have a dispute related to a law) involving more than $25,000 and many criminal cases (cases in which someone has broken the law). If one of the parties is not satisfied with the court's decision, they can appeal, or request a new trial, at a higher court called the court of appeals. Family courts handle cases involving children, divorce, adoption, and other family issues.

The state supreme court is the highest court in Michigan. The supreme court makes the final

MICHIGAN STATE GOVERNMENT

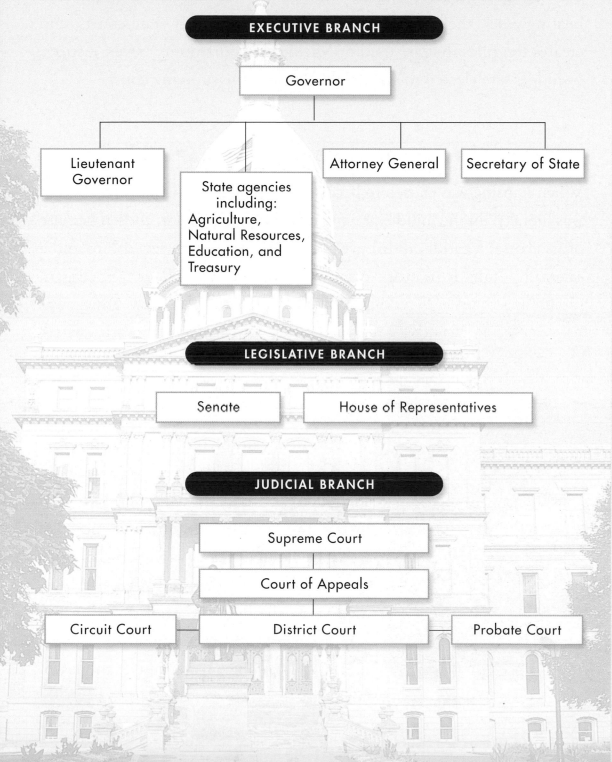

EXECUTIVE BRANCH

Governor

Lieutenant Governor

State agencies including: Agriculture, Natural Resources, Education, and Treasury

Attorney General

Secretary of State

LEGISLATIVE BRANCH

Senate

House of Representatives

JUDICIAL BRANCH

Supreme Court

Court of Appeals

Circuit Court

District Court

Probate Court

decision as to whether a lower court ruling was correct. In addition to hearing cases, the supreme court supervises the other state courts, and creates the rules that are used in Michigan's courtrooms. Seven justices, or judges, are elected to serve eight years on the supreme court.

TAKE A TOUR OF LANSING, THE CAPITAL CITY

When Lansing was chosen to become the capital of Michigan in 1847, it was literally "in the middle of nowhere." In fact, the spot, chosen because of its central location, didn't even have a name—just a few cabins and a sawmill. State legislators originally wanted to call it "Michigan, Michigan." Instead, the new town was named after Lansing, New York, where some of the first settlers were from. Almost overnight, a town sprang up that became the capital city.

Looking down from the top of the capitol dome, the floor of the rotunda appears to sink down in the center to form an upside-down dome.

The first capitol building was a white wooden building with green shutters and a small dome on top. It was replaced in 1879 by the present capitol, which is modeled after the United States capitol building in Washington, D.C. After more than one hundred years, the building needed repairs and improvements, and the capitol was restored in 1992. It is one of the best examples of

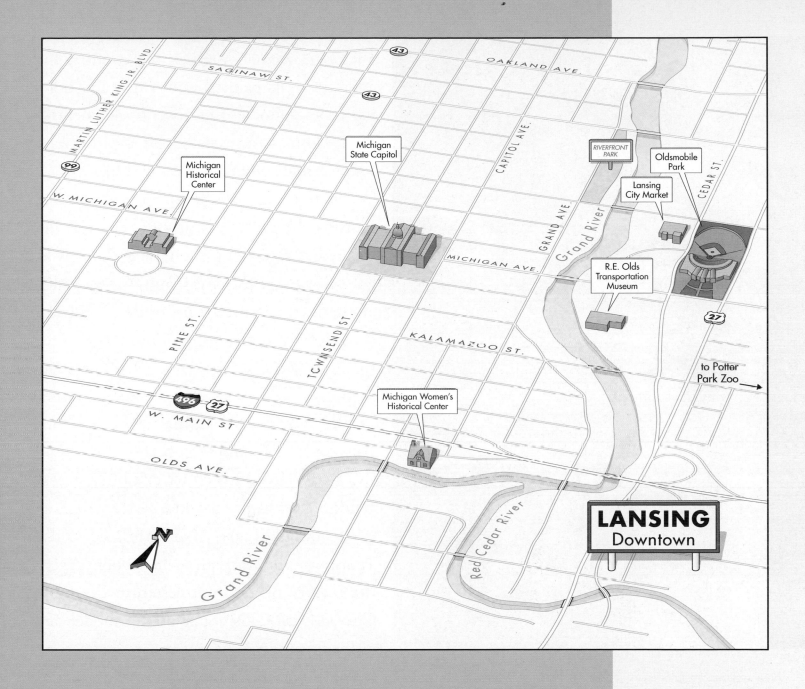

SAGINAW ST.

OAKLAND AVE.

MARTIN LUTHER KING JR. BLVD.

43

43

99

CAPITOL AVE.

Michigan
State Capitol

RIVERFRONT
PARK

Oldsmobile
Park

CEDAR ST.

Michigan
Historical
Center

Lansing
City Market

GRAND AVE.

Grand River

W. MICHIGAN AVE.

MICHIGAN AVE.

R.E. Olds
Transportation
Museum

27

PINE ST.

TOWNSEND ST.

KALAMAZOO ST.

to Potter
Park Zoo →

496   27

Michigan Women's
Historical Center

W. MAIN ST.

OLDS AVE.

Red Cedar River

LANSING
Downtown

N

Grand River

These visitors are taking a leisurely walk along the Grand River.

Victorian decorative art in the country. In addition to its painted wall panels and ceilings, the capitol also has twenty chandeliers made from cast metal. The capitol was restored to its original appearance in 1992.

There's a lot more to see and do in Lansing besides visiting the capitol. A steamboat ride along the Grand River is a good way to see the city. If you'd rather walk along the river, stop by historic Old Town's art galleries and antique stores. If you're there in either August or October you might also find yourself in the midst of one of Old Town's two annual festivals—the Lansing JazzFest and Octoberfest. Both festivals have live music, art exhibits, street vendors, and plenty of food.

If you like cars, visit the R.E. Olds Transportation Museum, where you can see the history of automobiles from the first Curved Dash Oldsmobile up to a model car of the future.

Potter Park Zoo may be small, but there's a lot to see and do there. Snow leopards, black rhinos, and timber wolves are just a few of the animals at Potter Park Zoo. You might also like to pack a picnic lunch, and after lunch take a ride on a camel or in a canoe.

At Oldsmobile Park there's something for everyone. Sports fans can watch the Lansing Lugnuts minor league baseball team in action. The park also hosts concerts, festivals, and evening movies.

Michigan State University is in neighboring East Lansing. The school was founded in 1855 as the first agricultural college in the United States. Today, over forty thousand students attend the college, and they study such varied subjects as medicine, engineering, and education, as well as agriculture. Michigan State is home to the 2000 NCAA championship men's basketball team, the MSU Spartans. The school also fields a college football team that has won two national titles. Two former Spartans, Herb Adderley and Joe DeLamielleure, later became members of the Pro Football Hall of Fame.

Lions are just one of the many animals at Potter Park Zoo.

CHAPTER FIVE

THE PEOPLE AND PLACES OF MICHIGAN

Visitors flock to Mackinac Island in the summer to enjoy its beautiful scenery.

More than ten million people live in Michigan. According to the U.S. Census Bureau's 2007 estimate, Michigan is home to 8,026,545 whites, 1,426,809 African Americans, 236,972 Asian Americans, and 50,474 Native Americans. Almost 400,000 Michiganders describe themselves as Hispanic or Latino.

More than one hundred different ethnic groups are represented in Michigan. Immigrants from Norway, Finland, and England came to Michigan in the 1840s. German, Dutch, Irish, and Polish immigrants arrived in the mid-1800s. While some African Americans moved to the state before and after the Civil War, many more came in the early 1900s, drawn by Henry Ford's promise to pay five dollars a day to his automobile factory workers. Mexican, Lebanese, and Polish immigrants also came to work in Michigan's factories.

In the twenty-first century, the fastest-growing groups include Hispanics, Asians, and Arabs. The greater Detroit area is home to the largest community of Arabs outside the Middle East. Similarly, the Polish community in Detroit has one of the largest Polish populations outside of Poland.

Michigan's original inhabitants, Native Americans, are now one of its smallest groups. Just five out of every 1,000 Michiganders are Native Americans.

The latest innovations in car design come from Michigan automobile companies.

WORKING IN MICHIGAN

Manufacturing, tourism, and agriculture are the top three industries in Michigan. When you think of Michigan, you think of cars. Three of the top manufacturers in the state are General Motors, Ford, and Chrysler. Their headquarters are all located in the southeastern part of the state.

Michigan manufacturing is more than cars (and car parts). Baby food, breakfast cereal, chemicals and medicine, furniture, home-cleaning products, refrigerators, sporting equipment, and paper are also produced in Michigan. You can probably find the names of many Michigan companies around your house: cleaning products from Amway, appliances from Whirlpool, breakfast cereals from Kellogg and Post, baby food from Gerber, and a recliner from La-Z-Boy. In addition to automobiles, the Detroit area produces steel, office equipment, rubber products, pharmaceuticals, and machine tool accessories.

Sending these goods to the rest of the world requires shipping. Detroit is one of the busiest inland ports in the world. Other ports such as Escanaba on Lake Michigan in the Upper Peninsula, Bay City on Lake Huron, and Ludington on Lake Michigan also serve Great Lakes freighters.

Tourism is Michigan's second largest industry. Tourism is the business of providing all the services needed to take care of people who come to visit the state, including hotels and motels, campgrounds, restaurants, shopping, recreation and entertainment, vehicles, and airlines. In state rankings for tourism, Michigan is number thirteen.

Michigan is a popular tourist area because it has something for everyone. Summer activities include boating, fishing, camping, swimming, and sightseeing. People enjoy Michigan's beaches, summer festivals, and museums. Its three national forests, six state forests, and 89 state parks are popular destinations for campers. In the fall, people enjoy driving the scenic highways and seeing the colorful autumn leaves. Winter tourism includes skiing, snowmobiling, snowboarding, and ice fishing. Michigan ranks first in the United States in the number of pleasure boat and snowmobile registrations, and in the number of golf courses there.

With more than fifty ski resorts, Michigan is a popular place for winter sports fans.

Michigan's major league sports teams generate lots of excitement, too. The Tigers (baseball), Lions (football), Pistons (basketball), and Red Wings (hockey) are all based in Detroit. College sports are also popular, especially with two "Big 10" colleges—Michigan State University and the University of Michigan—in the state. Many cities support regional and minor

EXTRA! EXTRA!

More than half of Michigan's tourists are people who already live there. According to a 1995 survey, tourists made 21.9 million trips in Michigan in 1994. Of those, 13.5 million were trips made by Michigan residents, while 8.4 million were made by people from out of state.

Wide receiver Calvin Johnson and other young stars have made the Detroit Lions a more exciting football team than ever.

league baseball, soccer, and hockey teams, too.

Agriculture is Michigan's third largest industry. You could fill an entire grocery cart just by choosing foods grown in Michigan. The state leads the nation in production of tart cherries, blueberries, navy beans, and pickling cucumbers. It ranks in the top ten for growing apples and grapes and producing milk and ice cream. Celery, asparagus, and spearmint are also important crops in Michigan. Some of the state's field crops include oats, hay, corn, potatoes, and soybeans. Many residents in the Thumb are farmers. The main crops in this part of the state are sugar beets, navy beans, and grain. Some farmers raise livestock such as cattle, sheep, and pigs. Michigan is also a top producer of geraniums and Christmas trees.

This Michigan farmer is checking on his young pigs.

MINN.

Lake Superior

CANADA

ONTARIO

0   25   50 mi.

0   25   50 km

Marquette

N

WISCONSIN

Lake Michigan

Lake Huron

Berries

Cattle

Copper

Corn

Dairy

Fish

Fruit

Grapes

Hay

Hogs

Iron ore

Limestone

Manufacturing

Natural Gas

Oats

Petroleum

Potatoes

Poultry

Salt

Sheep

Soybeans

Tourism

Vegetables

Wheat

Grand Rapids

Lansing

Flint

Detroit

ILL.

INDIANA

OHIO

Lake Erie

54

Western Upper Peninsula

The western part of the Upper Peninsula is the farthest corner of the state. In the Porcupine and Huron Mountains you'll find some of the best skiing in Michigan. The U.S. National Ski and Snowboard Hall of Fame and Museum in Ishpeming shows the history of skiing in Michigan and the United States. Photographs, antique skis, a cable car, and trophies from skiing champions are on display.

The U.S. National Ski and Snowboard Hall of Fame tells the stories of famous skiers and ski history.

Isle Royale National Park, located off the coast of Keweenaw Peninsula in Lake Superior, is Michigan's only national park. The island's rugged shores, forests, and lakes are a great place for hiking, fishing, and camping. Be on the lookout for wolves and moose!

Several museums and mining tours remind visitors of the state's mining heritage. Coppertown U.S.A. in Calumet has a model mine and displays of mining equipment. The Iron Mountain Iron Mine takes visitors on a train ride that includes demonstrations of mining machinery.

The two largest cities in this part of Michigan are Marquette and Escanaba. Marquette is the shopping and medical center of the region, and also the home of Northern Michigan University. Freighters regularly leave Escanaba with iron ore and timber for manufacturing.

Eastern Upper Peninsula

The two oldest settlements in the state are in the eastern Upper Peninsula. St. Ignace, founded in 1671, is the site of the Father Marquette National Memorial. Sault Ste. Marie is the oldest and largest city in the eastern Upper Peninsula. It was founded in 1668. One of the greatest mechanical wonders in the state—the Soo Locks—is also a popular tourist attraction in this area. Built in 1855, the locks enable ships to pass from Lake Superior to Lake Huron along the St. Marys River. More than 95 million tons of freight pass through the locks every year. The eastern Upper Peninsula is also home to the Bay Mills Chippewa Reservation in Brimley and the Sault Ste. Marie Chippewa Reservation.

This region is known for its natural wonders. The Pictured Rocks National Lakeshore and Hiawatha National Forest offer camping, hiking, fishing, and sightseeing. Seney National Wildlife Refuge, the largest wildlife refuge east of the Mississippi River, provides a safe haven to wolves, deer, bears, moose, coyotes, and Canada geese.

The Mackinac Bridge, sometimes called "Mighty Mac," is the only link between the upper and lower peninsulas. This 5-mile (8-km) long suspension bridge was built in 1957. It is one of the longest bridges of its type in the world.

A ship sits high in the Soo Locks, waiting for the water level to drop so it can travel from Lake Superior to Lake Huron.

It took 3,500 people, 1,000,000 steel bolts, and 42,000 miles (67,592 km) of wire to build the Mackinac Bridge.

Mackinaw City and Mackinac Island

Mackinaw City is on the southern side of the Mackinac Bridge. From here you can take the ferry to Mackinac Island, a resort town where cars are not allowed. Horse-drawn carriages or bicycles take visitors to Fort Mackinac, where costumed guides reenact life in a military fort during the 1700s. Another historic site, Fort Michilimackinac, was built by the French in 1715. In addition to the fort, you can visit a priest's house, a blacksmith shop, a French church, and a British trader's house.

Northwest Michigan

Fruit-growing and tourism are the main industries along the northern Lake Michigan coastline. Traverse City is the cherry capital of the world. Every year, Traverse City hosts the National Cherry Festival that

Michigan produces more red tart cherries than any other state.

Cherries and apples are abundant in Michigan's orchards, and Kellogg's cereals are an important part of Michigan's history and economy. This easy recipe combines these foods in one mouthwatering dessert. Don't forget to ask an adult for help!

CHERRY-APPLE CRISP

1 can (21 oz.) tart cherry pie filling
1 can (21 oz.) apple pie filling
1 teaspoon apple pie spice
3 cups Kellogg's Rice Krispies® cereal
1/4 cup firmly packed brown sugar
1 tablespoon butter
3 tablespoons light corn syrup

1. Preheat oven to 350°F.
2. Combine pie fillings and apple pie spice. Spread evenly in 12 x 7 x 2-inch (two-quart) glass baking dish. Set aside.
3. In a large bowl, thoroughly combine the remaining ingredients. Sprinkle evenly over the filling mixture.
4. Bake for thirty minutes or until the filling bubbles around the edges and the cereal starts to brown. Serve warm or cold, with whipped topping or frozen yogurt.

includes a parade, foods made from cherries, and athletic events. Both summer and winter resorts are dotted throughout the area—tourists can visit Sleeping Bear Dunes National Lakeshore, ski at Boyne Mountain, or go boating on one of the many inland lakes.

The Eastern Edge

Alpena, on Lake Huron, is known as "cement city." The limestone quarries here and in Rogers City provide raw materials for cement. Tourists also visit Alpena to see the lighthouses, go boating and fishing in Thunder Bay, and dive in Lake Huron.

Midland, Saginaw, and Bay City make up what is known as the tri-city area. In Saginaw, stop by the Saginaw Art Museum, where visitors can try their hand at creating different types of art. Midland is the headquarters of Dow Chemical Corporation. Tourists can visit Dow Gardens, a 110-acre (45-ha) garden where a wide variety of flowers and plants grow. Exhibits in the Herbert H. Dow Historical Museum follow the life of Herbert Dow, a pioneering chemist and founder of Dow Chemical. Bay City is an important center of commerce, industry, government, and culture on the eastern edge.

The Thumb

Michigan's Thumb region features 90 miles (145 km) of lakeshore, where tourists can visit small museums, lighthouses, and beaches. Stop and see Native American carvings, called

FIND OUT MORE

Make your own rock carvings. With help from an adult, mix and pour plaster of paris into a shoebox lid. When it hardens, use colored chalk to draw pictures and symbols on your "rock."

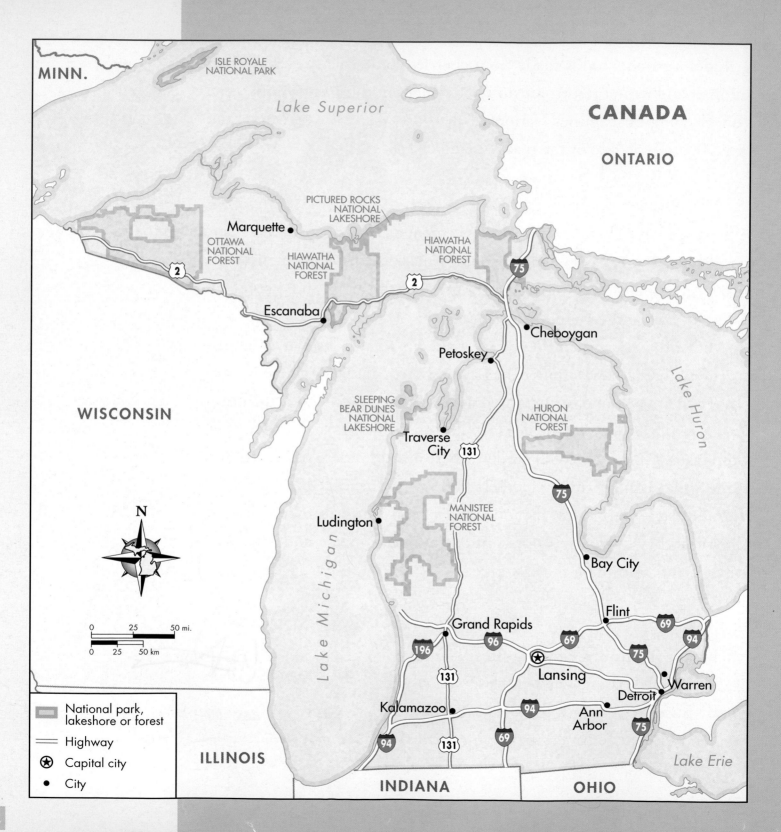

MINN.

ISLE ROYALE
NATIONAL PARK

Lake Superior

CANADA

ONTARIO

PICTURED ROCKS
NATIONAL
LAKESHORE

Marquette

OTTAWA
NATIONAL
FOREST

HIAWATHA
NATIONAL
FOREST

HIAWATHA
NATIONAL
FOREST

2

75

Escanaba

Cheboygan

Petoskey

WISCONSIN

SLEEPING
BEAR DUNES
NATIONAL
LAKESHORE

Lake Huron

HURON
NATIONAL
FOREST

Traverse
City

131

N

MANISTEE
NATIONAL
FOREST

75

Ludington

Bay City

Lake Michigan

Flint

69

0   25   50 mi.

0   25   50 km

Grand Rapids

96

69

75

94

196

131

Lansing

94

Warren

National park,
lakeshore or forest

Kalamazoo

Detroit

Highway

Ann
Arbor

75

Capital city

City

ILLINOIS

94

131

69

Lake Erie

INDIANA

OHIO

the Sanilac Petroglyphs, in Bad Axe. They are between 400 and 1,000 years old. The petroglyphs, which include pictures of mythical water panthers, deer, and an archer, show what life was like for the woodland people who once lived in the Thumb area.

Port Huron is the Thumb's largest city. It is part of what is known as the "Blue Water Area," where sailing and boating are popular activities. Port Huron is also the childhood home of inventor Thomas Edison.

These sailboats on Lake Huron create a picture-perfect water scene.

(opposite)
The Detroit skyline sparkles at night.

Southeastern Michigan

Almost half the state's population lives in Wayne, Oakland, and Macomb counties, located in and around Detroit. Detroit is the largest city in Michigan and the tenth largest city in the United States.

There is so much to see and do in Detroit. All of the state's major league sports teams play in Detroit. The Motown Historical Museum pays tribute to the African-American record company founded by Berry Gordy in 1959. An elevated railway called the People Mover travels through the downtown area, where one of the world's tallest buildings, the Renaissance Center, is located.

Just outside Detroit in Dearborn is Greenfield Village, a huge open-air museum with nearly one hundred historic buildings. Here you can see the laboratories of Thomas Edison and the Wright Brothers, as well as a courthouse where Abraham Lincoln once practiced law. The nearby Henry Ford Museum's collection includes old stagecoaches, early television sets, and the world's first successful helicopter.

West of Detroit is Ann Arbor, home to the University of Michigan—the first state university in the United States. Ann Arbor also has world-renowned medical facilities, and one of the country's most popular summer art festivals.

WHO'S WHO IN MICHIGAN?

Dennis Archer (1942–) served as a justice on the Michigan Supreme Court for five years before being elected mayor of Detroit in 1993. Under his leadership, Detroit was able to attract new businesses and reduce crime. Archer served as mayor until 2001. He was born in Detroit.

Michigan's heartland has rolling hills and fertile fields that attracted many of the state's early settlers. After the Detroit metro area, this region has most of the state's larger cities, including Grand Rapids, Lansing, Jackson, Kalamazoo, and Battle Creek.

Visit the Kalamazoo Aviation History Museum to see rare airplanes from before World War I, a flight simulator, and daily flying demonstrations. At Battle Creek's Cereal City U.S.A. you can find out how breakfast cereal is made, learn the history of cereal, and create a cereal box with your face on it. The Michigan Space and Science Center in Jackson

The Michigan Space and Science center contains artifacts from all of America's space programs.

features lunar rocks, a moon rover, spacesuits, and a model of the Hubble Space Telescope.

The tiny town of Colon is "the Magic Capital of the World." Abbott's Magic Company, the world's largest producer of handmade magical illusions, is in Colon. The store sponsors an annual summer convention for professional and amateur magicians.

Soaring Eagle Casino, where people can gamble, see shows, and eat at restaurants, is operated by members of the Isabella Chippewa Reservation in Mt. Pleasant. The casino has helped to raise money for Native American tribes to provide services such as health care, schools, and law enforcement.

Lake Michigan Coast

The lakeshore is the heart of Michigan tourism, with miles of beaches, antique shops, and resorts. Towns along the coast include St. Joseph, South Haven, Saugatuck, Muskegon, Grand Haven, and Ludington. Saugatuck is an art colony with many unique shops. In South Haven, you can participate in a pie-eating contest or enjoy a blueberry pancake breakfast at the National Blueberry Festival every summer. The lake effect from Lake Michigan provides ideal growing conditions for many berry farms, orchards, and vineyards.

At Ludington, tourists can take a four-hour ferry ride across Lake Michigan to Manitowoc, Wisconsin on the S.S. *Badger*. You can relax while you're on the ferry and visit the ship's museum, watch live

entertainment, or play in a video arcade. You can also go on deck and watch the waves as you cross the sixty miles (97 km) of Lake Michigan.

From forests to cities, and automobiles to apples, the Great Lakes State has something for everyone.

MICHIGAN ALMANAC

Statehood date and number: January 26, 1837, the 26th state

State seal: Adopted 1911. An elk and a moose on either side of a shield, which shows a sun rising over a lake and a man standing on a peninsula with one hand raised in peace and the other holding a rifle. An eagle is above the shield. Three Latin phrases are on the shield: *Tuebor* ("I will defend"), *E pluribus unum* ("Out of many, one"), and *Si quaeris peninsulam amoenam, circumspice* ("If you seek a pleasant peninsula, look about you").

State flag: Adopted 1911. Blue with the state coat of arms on both sides.

Geographic center: St. Louis is the "middle of the mitten," the geographic center of the lower peninsula; Gaylord is the center of the entire state

Total area/rank: 96,716 square miles (250,494 sq km)/11th

Coastline: 3,288 miles (5,292 km)

Borders: Lake Michigan, Wisconsin, Canada, Lake Huron, Lake Erie, Lake Superior, Ohio, and Indiana

Latitude and longitude: Michigan is approximately between 41° 41' and 48° 18' N and 82° 7' and 90° 25' W.

Highest/lowest elevation: Mount Arvon, 1,979 feet (603 meters)/Lake Erie, 572 feet (175 m)

Hottest/coldest temperature: 112° Fahrenheit (44.4° Celsius) in Mio on July 13, 1936/ −51°F (−46.1°C) in Vanderbilt on February 9, 1934 (both in the Upper Peninsula)

Land area/rank: 56,804 square miles (147,121 sq km)/22nd

Inland water area: 1,611 square miles (4,172 sq km)

Population/rank: 9,938,444 (2000 census)/8th

Population of major cities:

   Detroit: 951,270

   Grand Rapids: 197,800

   Warren: 138,247

   Flint: 124,943

   Lansing: 119,128

Origin of state name: *Michi-gama*, Algonquian word for "big (or great) water" or a Chippewa word *Majigan* for "clearing"

State capital: Lansing

Previous capitals: Detroit (until 1847)

Counties: 83

State government: 38 senators, 110 representatives

Major lakes/rivers: Major lakes (other than the Great Lakes): Burt, Gogebic, Higgins, Houghton, Manistique, Mullet/Major rivers: St. Marys, Detroit, Grand, Muskegon, Au Sable, St. Clair, and St. Joseph

Farm products: Tart cherries, blueberries, apples, dried beans, pickling cucumbers, Christmas trees, lilies, geraniums, wheat, oats, hay, corn, rye, potatoes, soybeans, and sugar beets

Livestock: Cattle/calves, sheep/lambs, hogs/pigs, chickens

Manufactured products: Automobiles, paper products, pharmaceuticals, chemicals, baby food, cereal, refrigerators, and furniture

Mining products: Iron ore, copper, limestone, gypsum, salt, petroleum, and natural gas

Fishing products: Trout, salmon, bluegill, perch, large and smallmouth bass, pike, and whitefish

Bird: Robin

Fish: Brook trout

Flower: Apple blossom

Game mammal: White-tailed deer

Gem: Chlorastrolite (Isle Royale greenstone)

Motto: *Si quaeris peninsulam amoenam, circumspice.* (If you seek a pleasant peninsula, look about you.)

Nicknames: Great Lakes State, Wolverine State, Water Wonderland

Reptile: Painted turtle

Soil: Kalkaska sand

Song: "Michigan, My Michigan" (sung to the tune of "O Tannenbaum"), written by William Otto Miessner and Douglas M. Malloch

Stone: Petoskey stone

Tree: White pine

Wildlife: White-tailed deer, black bear, moose, raccoon, red fox, squirrel, beaver, rabbit, porcupine, elk, blue heron, kingfisher, ducks, gulls, partridge, pheasant, and turkey

Wildflower: Dwarf lake iris

TIMELINE

MICHIGAN STATE HISTORY

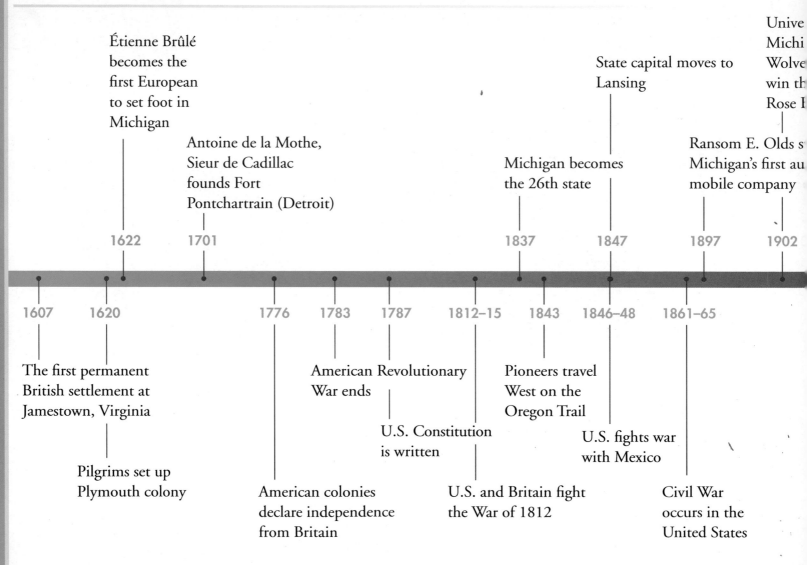

Étienne Brûlé becomes the first European to set foot in Michigan

Antoine de la Mothe, Sieur de Cadillac founds Fort Pontchartrain (Detroit)

State capital moves to Lansing

Unive
Michi
Wolve
win th
Rose I

Michigan becomes the 26th state

Ransom E. Olds s
Michigan's first au
mobile company

1622   **1701**   **1837**   **1847**   **1897**   **1902**

1607   **1620**   **1776**   **1783**   **1787**   **1812–15**   **1843**   **1846–48**   **1861–65**

The first permanent British settlement at Jamestown, Virginia

American Revolutionary War ends

Pioneers travel West on the Oregon Trail

U.S. Constitution is written

U.S. fights war with Mexico

Pilgrims set up Plymouth colony

American colonies declare independence from Britain

U.S. and Britain fight the War of 1812

Civil War occurs in the United States

UNITED STATES HISTORY

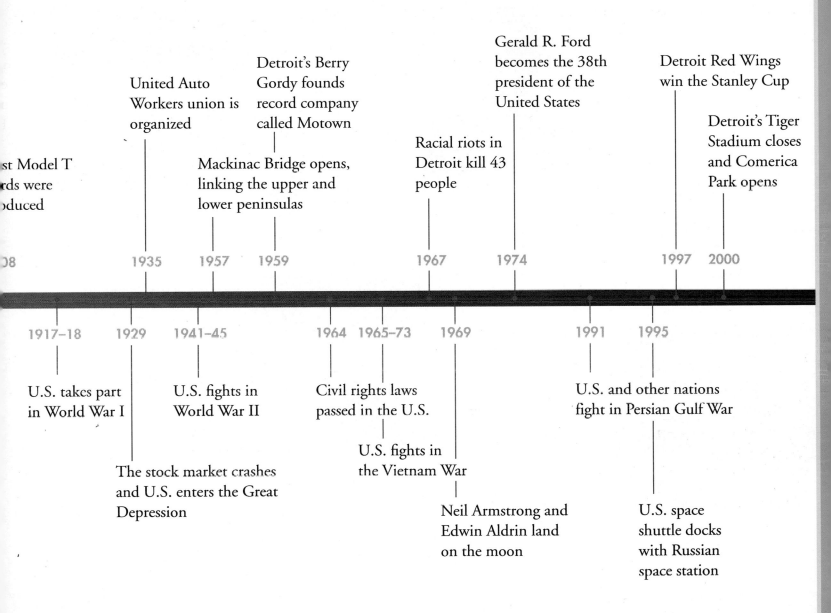

st Model T
rds were
oduced

United Auto
Workers union is
organized

Detroit's Berry
Gordy founds
record company
called Motown

Mackinac Bridge opens,
linking the upper and
lower peninsulas

Gerald R. Ford
becomes the 38th
president of the
United States

Racial riots in
Detroit kill 43
people

Detroit Red Wings
win the Stanley Cup

Detroit's Tiger
Stadium closes
and Comerica
Park opens

08   1935   1957   1959   1967   1974   1997   2000

1917–18   1929   1941–45   1964 1965–73 1969   1991   1995

U.S. takes part
in World War I

U.S. fights in
World War II

Civil rights laws
passed in the U.S.

U.S. and other nations
fight in Persian Gulf War

The stock market crashes
and U.S. enters the Great
Depression

U.S. fights in
the Vietnam War

Neil Armstrong and
Edwin Aldrin land
on the moon

U.S. space
shuttle docks
with Russian
space station

GALLERY OF FAMOUS MICHIGANIANS

Ralph J. Bunche (1904–1971)
Statesman who helped to found the United Nations, an organization that works for peace throughout the world. He was the first African-American to win the Nobel Peace Prize (1950). Born in Detroit.

Charles Lindbergh (1902–1974)
Aviator. In 1927 he made the first solo airplane flight across the Atlantic Ocean in his plane, *The Spirit of St. Louis.* Born in Detroit.

Will Carleton (1845–1912)
Poet laureate of Michigan. He is best known for his poems about rural life. His most famous poem, "Over the Hill to the Poorhouse," called national attention to problems facing elderly and homeless people in the late 1800s. He was born in Hillsdale.

Jerry Linenger (1955–)
NASA astronaut. He spent 132 days in space aboard the Russian Space Station Mir in 1997. Born in Mt. Clemens.

Edna Ferber (1885–1968)
Pulitzer Prize-winning author. Considered one of the finest U.S. novelists of her day. Born in Kalamazoo.

Joe Louis (1914–1981)
Professional boxer in the 1930s and 1940s. He was the heavyweight champion of the world for twelve years, starting in 1937. Born in Alabama and grew up in Detroit.

Chris Van Allsburg (1949–)
Award winning author-illustrator whose books include *Jumanji* and *The Polar Express.* Born in Grand Rapids.

Earvin "Magic" Johnson (1959–)
NBA basketball player for the Los Angeles Lakers. Before joining the Lakers he played with Michigan State University's Spartans, leading them to win the NCAA tournament in 1979. Born in Lansing.

Bertha Van Hoosen (1863–1952)
Surgeon. Founder and first president of the American Medical Women's Association in 1917. Born in Rochester Hills.

GLOSSARY

abolitionist: person who worked to end slavery in the United States in the 1800s

arsenal: building for manufacturing or storing military equipment or weapons

cargo: load or freight carried by a ship

colonize: to settle a new land outside the home country that is ruled by the home country

Confederacy: name for the states that broke away from the United States and formed their own government during the Civil War

contaminate: to infect or pollute

discrimination: preferential treatment (usually used to describe unfavorable treatment) given to a person or class of people

ethnic: relating to large groups of people with common racial, national, tribal, religious, or cultural origin

geologist: scientist who studies the earth

glacier: large body of ice moving slowly down a slope or valley or spreading outward on a land surface

immigrant: person who comes to a country from another to become a permanent resident

labor union: organization of workers formed to improve wages, benefits, and working conditions for its members

lake effect: a weather pattern that causes snowfall or rainfall, in which cold air picks up water vapor as it moves over a warm lake, then releases this moisture downwind of shore

mastodon: type of extinct mammal resembling an elephant with long, curved tusks

peninsula: body of land bordered on three sides by water

pharmaceutical: relating to the manufacture and sale of medicinal drugs

reef: irregular mass, strip, or ridge of rock or coral that rises close to the surface of a body of water

reservation: area of land set aside for the use of Native Americans

rural: relating to the countryside

surveyor: person whose job is to map land areas

tourism: business of providing food, entertainment, and housing for visitors

treaty: agreement or contract in writing between two or more governing bodies

Underground Railroad: system of cooperation among antislavery people in the United States by which enslaved Africans were secretly helped to reach the North or Canada

urban: relating to a city or city life

voyageur: person employed by a fur company to transport goods and people to and from trading posts

FOR MORE INFORMATION

Websites

Michigan Kids!
http://www.michigan.gov/kids
Contains information about Michigan's history, places to visit, and more.

Michigan Government
http://www.cantonpl.org/kids/mgov.html
Kid-friendly links to information about the government of Michigan and the state's elected officals.

Michigan.gov
http://www.michigan.gov
The official portal to all things Michigan.

Books

Doherty, Craig A. and Katherine M. Doherty. *The Erie Canal (Building America)*. Woodbridge, CT: Blackbirch Press, 1996.

Epstein, Rachel. *W.K. Kellogg: Generous Genius (Community Builders)*. Danbury, CT: Children's Press, 2000.

Gourley, Catherine. *Wheels of Time: A Biography of Henry Ford*. Brookfield, CT: Millbrook Press, 1997.

Addresses

Michigan Historical Center
717 W. Allegan St.
Lansing, MI 48933

Travel Michigan
2nd Floor Victor Center
201 N. Washington Square
Lansing, MI 48913

Governor Jennifer M. Granholm
P.O. Box 30013
Lansing, MI 48909

INDEX

MEET THE AUTHOR

Elizabeth M. Johnson is a writer and public relations manager in Lansing, Michigan. She, her husband, and their three sons have lived in Michigan since 1995. Johnson knew her children were true Michiganians when her oldest son pointed to a spot on his right hand to show someone where he lived. Some of her favorite places in Michigan are Greenfield Village in Dearborn, Sleeping Bear Dunes, and the Michigan Space and Science Center in Jackson.

Photographs © 2009: AP Images/J. Kyle Keener/Detroit Free Press: 64; Archives of Labor and Urban Affairs, Wayne State University: 35; Corbis Images: 63 (James L. Amos), 57 (Lowell Georgia), 48 (Mark Gibson), 74 top right (Hulton-Deutsch Collection), 8 (Layne Kennedy), 16 (Lake County Museum), 74 top left (David Lees), 34 (Museum of Flight), cover (Phil Schermeister), 42 (Allan Tannenbaum), 74 bottom left (Underwood & Underwood), 36 (UPI), 22, 28 bottom, 33; Dembinsky Photo Assoc.: 3 left, 7 (Terry Donnelly), 12 (Barbara Gerlach); Detroit Public Library, Burton Historical Collection: 24; Getty Images: 31 (Archive Photos), 52 (Scott Boehm), 49 (Jeff Corwin/Stone), 28 top (Hulton Getty Picture Collection/Stone), 74 bottom right (Hulton-Deutsch Collection/AllSport USA), 71 bottom right (Bill Ivy/Stone), 4, 44, 65, 68 (Vito Palmisano/Stone), 53 (Andy Sacks/Stone), 3 right, 58 (Phil Schermeister/Stone); Jim West: 46; MapQuest.com, Inc.: 70; Martin Hintz: 51; Michigan Space and Science Center: 67; Midwestock/Eric R. Berndt: 15; North Wind Picture Archives: 17, 18, 29; Potter Park Zoological Society/David B. Mills, East Lansing: 47; Richard W. Clark: 13; Robertstock.com/W. Janoud: 71 left; Stock Montage, Inc.: 19, 27; Superstock, Inc.: 23 (Culver Pictures), 20, 25; Traverse City C.V.B.: 59; Unicorn Stock Photos: 37 (Chris Boylan), 71 top right (Ted Rose); Visuals Unlimited: 11 (Ross Frid), 55 (Mark E. Gibson), 39, 43 background (Cheryl Hogue); www.lifestylelaboratory.com: 30.

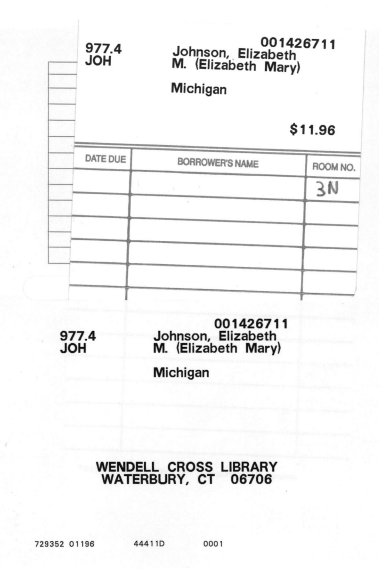

977.4
JOH

001426711
Johnson, Elizabeth
M. (Elizabeth Mary)

Michigan

$11.96

DATE DUE	BORROWER'S NAME	ROOM NO.
		3N